PERFUME OF
THE INJURED

E. R. BEIRNE

To my Mother, who read to me.

To my sons, Desmond & Colin
for their unconditional love.

To those who inspired me,
the kind, the unkind, and my beloved absent.

TABLE OF CONTENTS

TABLE OF CONTENTS – *Cont'd*

BIRTHDAY POEMS

THE LAST POEMS FOR MY FATHER

Acts of Random Kindness
Happiness in These Times

Some times
the happiness that
surges thru me
electricity plus
spills out
all over someone else

San Salvador or
Guatemala
The South American family in line
before me with their purchase
I never would have noticed
except for the dark silent daughter
holding the white patent leather
handbag up
for her mother's approval

This happiness
is physical
It upsets my lower intestines
Causes anxiety and fear
It's manic and genuine and full
of the sound of ringing
the bells

This intention
Coming in like
cosmic dust or
ray beam
Moves in over us
from me to you
a tidal wave of great heart

The line of payment shifts

Silent and closed
Tired or poor
Lack of empathy
or indifferent knowing
Mother daughter scenario
plays out

No response
Daughter understands
Silently the cup of expectation
empties
She put the handbag back where she
found it
Columbus left the new world

I look all around
No one saw this exchange
It all continues on

Something is moving in me and moving me
I am gearing up for the easily explained
The chatty and numb hold their wallets
Wait their turns

I was next in line
Jumping up and down inside
Do it! The eternal flow said
They were leaving slowly
-I was next in line
The heavy sadness of missing my chance
had me running up to the mother
then to the display shelf
I bought the handbag and ran back after the girl

No one was prepared for this expectation
Not even me
The young girl looked me right in the eye
The channel was open
A miracle might have occurred

if we'd known what to do or say
We might have ended something ugly and all too human

The giving
The receiving
The patent leather metaphor for all we lack
We hugged
For little more than 30 seconds
We could love each other

No Name for It

We taught each other almost nothing
over the years
He showed me the face of selfishness
I shot back
with a cold glass of resentment

We were an even match
Insecurity flaming
We held our palms over the wick
and sizzled inside

Nearing the end
we held each other
in low self esteem

I held him high
on the sharp pinnacle of alcohol abuse
and reckless irresponsibility
Emotional absence slapped me in the face
over and over

He pinned me into a similar corner
We wore the red dunce cap
and suffocated under the manipulations
sins of omission
lives unshared

Absent and unknowable
and so far removed
The midlife crisis ate him whole
Sutured for youth
Traveling alone
while the reservations said two

"He was never there"
goes the litany
"I love you, now go away"

Like ugly plants
We grew apart and died dry
"It seems like a dream"
I say this now
Someone told me their mother said that

It seemed fitting so I wear it.
It is part of the eulogy
for our unbearable lack of union

Not right but wrong from the get go
Waiting for the car in the driveway
For the other shoe to drop
For the fool on the hill
whose father beat him relentlessly
until he made a run for it

Intimacy and denial
Come close move away

Before and after each tall glass of something good

We limped away from the mirror
We fell through
Together
The ugly nest of
who did what to whom is empty
Looking back on the destructions
Wiping the shards from our hair

No More

Take this sadness
This fat wrapped
around my heart

Take this
White noise
of the tragic spheres

Juggle it somewhere else
Over another head

Orbit elsewhere
The teary muse
of my pondering

The science fiction
of what might have been

I am still in love with my memories
The story I re-wrote daily
All about you
when you were never there

The fiction
I concocted
about your ways and days

and my role as the victim
well played

Until truth
That savage bite
Ripped me away
from my
Ropes and shafts

New Year's

Eminent sparkle
The white of the eye, the metallic taste on the bud, all things so great with atomic
weight ready to deploy and entropy at the drop of a ball from a great height in a
great big city.

The next thing is the next thing as it unravels in the revel and the revealing of the
real deal the best foot to put forward is usually on the right side or the stronger of
the two or the four or the six,   tick tock the happy cheer edicts.

Imminent presence
A tunnel hurtling towards a lunging forth a perking brew
These are the things I wish for you
Love in the gut food for the soul solely meant to help you
with its harmfulness

The big bang is now recognized
As just another wakeup call

My how time whizzes through the cosmos as if we are it.
As if we meant it as if we are the end all be all of whatever existence shrieks out
in the silences.

Sit Down

There is a dry purge
that goes on and on
As the seasons shift
and the memories change
their tune and color

A tender rustle
A sore rearrangement
of the limbs
The tentacles
The oblivion

Mothers
and tender lambs
All grown up
drink wine together

This is not ritual
or appeasement
For the orange souls
of young and old

This is the grape
The harvest
The pressing down
Until we bleed
and bear fruit

This is the cup that
runs away
with the blessing

Soul Mate

My singular existence interrupted
by the silver threads of connection
and voice

I miss voice
Someone asking me where they might have put something
or if I want a glass of wine

I miss the physicality of connection
A leg hefted over my thigh
The silk of skin
Advancing physical pleasure
in the dark of the night

I've had most of this
Friendship without intimacy
Sex without connection of spirit

And I wanted all of it
The soul to soul
The heart to heart
And now
as an aging relic
I want it even more so

Where is a heart
That can stand so close to another
That we beat in rhythm?

Murderers

How can it be?
That murderers

Mothers who tie their babies to the toilet
Partnered gun lovers
Coupled kidnappers of young girls
Women who initiate and share
or stand by their man
Watching, helping, egging on

While molestation
Devastation and psychic destruction
weep from their pores
like the sweat of hell

How is it
That these kinds of sickness
can sustain loyal relationships
with significant others

While I
am always alone

And work so hard
for kindness?

A Gated Community

In the hot suburbs
years ago
when the spring in my step
levitated my soul
I had a garden gate

Created by three men
one who never loved me
the two others
who loved me no more
by the garden gate

The gate of moon and star
was hewn from the pine
by an unloving one
Laser cut
by anger, by grandiosity and chemical fumes
so necessary to all his creations

The slats were received
The moon slat and the 5 pointed star slat
The gate flat in the grass
and the slats nailed in
Wrist and ankle they were slapped in
Haphazard and slow
by one who no longer loved me
No longer loved

He slapped them in
Replaced the fence and moved on
The fence held fast
till the next owner swung it both ways

And the dark man
The unknown man
who built the original gate

From wood he was given
From dollars he was given
Never knowing
the history of
the lives

The gate held back

Holy Chasm

Today strange vibes
are in this church office
I meter and intuit
Never fully catching the meaning

But today
Strange flat waves of unstructured humanity
shift around this office space

The organized religion
that draws them in
is losing its grip
its yoke and harness
Medieval vernaculars
Mediocre society
and rigid courtesies
have sprung a leak

Soon these people might be free

A gush of frustrated exclamation
from the Monsignor
coughing and hacking down the hallway
Silent except for the whipping ventilation
spreading germs

A wrinkle in the sands of time
has hit the pink Bermuda shore
of religion today

Ten years… or Eleven

A myriad of matchstick partners
with heads of crimson ignition flare
then narrow towards the horizon

Ten years after the dissolution
of the union of souls
Or only bodies, who really knows
I burn daily with the iron brand
of regrets and the bitter tongue
Still taut and unrolling the
oils of forgiveness

The old words and there were only a few
Widely spaced and wicked
How they sliced apart the heart
The heart of the matter
The matter with you
The excellent beginnings when I wrote I love you
backwards on your forehead in the woods
on the mountainside upstate

Such a match
Lit the candles for our sons
And our fathers
And then blackened and smoking
became as difficult as Normandy for one or two

Every day you come into my house
standing mute and cemented
behind my soul
and wait in the same matchbox
where I sit and then stand and then sit
and rant and cry out
the flare and flicker of my
self-made miseries

And the burning
Oh, the burning
Paradox and irony are oxygen
In this place

and the
friction between love and disappointment
that sheds no light nor boundary

A little flame
A little blame

Repairman Repair

Even the dog has failed
and sleeps all day

The drug of choice is sugar
and ice water
and plenty of it
Till death pounds on the interior arteries
Requesting let me in
to the flux and flow

I rode south
to scour the dirt
for shiny bits of possibility
And ended the day
gnawing at fatty turkey tails
tucked between my thighs
as my greasy hands drove north

I am numbed by my expectations
Relieved by the indifferent ugliness
all around me
Desperate to be away from
the spiky radiating energies
of the narcissist, of the hell bent
and the self-righteous
Each a box of poison
waiting for a fling
in the right direction

Our culture is a miserable scorpion
Half crushed and bellowing

A sin filled self-made requiem

Mortgaged

She wears her position
in the office of sighs
like a buffalo skin

Aims when she sees weakness
A big woman
with a hurt cherub face
Bruised lips
Raccoon eyes ringed and bound
directly to a harness around the heart

Mind like a shark

She is practiced and attuned
to maneuver and function
The natural rhythms
do not call to her
Tall and broad
A Rodin woman, on the move
She wants to "kill her kids"

The office is filled with exes
Young "I don't know what"
I wanna bees
One guy clips by
snapping his fingers
His energy is sharp
and badly dressed

Another one
He rules the roost
Golf shirt, boating shoes
He's making it happen

Up at the reception desk
Three bowls of artificial flowers

progressively enlarge
in position
around the room
This is the home of the
"Thinking Mortgage"

The openings and
closings of the thick glass door
causes everyone to look up

We all enter into possibility
Some wearing armor
Others falling apart behind steel desks

And the upscale clientele, so perfectly healthy
Raised in perfection to perfect delight

This is where understanding fails me
I just don't get it

The sun is always shining
Lemons become lemonade
The bright side
moves as fast as I do
Always just one step ahead
of where I want to be

I want to be
Full throttle
Ahead of where I was
Entering the next possibility
Minus the loan officers
Monday Morning at my Desk

After all
I am still receptive and accepting
at the reception desk

She comes to me
with e-mails in hand
Tearful and unconscious
of what set in motion
The destiny
of her love

I saw it coming
The more she gave
the less she got
the harder she tried
to move the masculine mountain
the heavier the rock became

But she carries it still
on her back
Uphill all the way
And like a good girl
she smiles and smiles

And pours blue martinis
into her hunched over soul

Filled with the pain
of making it all work out

I have been there myself
Waiting
Awake at night
For the right answer
in the wrong circumstances

Hope and imagination
My religion
Pouring balm and life onto
the wilt of
what never grew

She is so sweet and giving

How can I tell her

That the only way to move a mountain
is to cut it down
Slice it apart
with the big machinations

Until it is not
a mountain anymore

Just a molehill
she can crawl inside of
to lick the wounds of love

Roadwork

Driving there
is a gentle measurement
as the trees clip by

Breath is paced
Steering angles and dips
riding a dark hard wave
of asphalt and salt

Out at the horizon
there could be cactus spines
or variegated ropes
of tropical vine and memory

Who knows?
If you stretch the horizon far enough
it encompasses everything

Stretch that horizon line
That vista of imagination

and the highway becomes
an undulating Jello
dipping and swinging its sinuous length

towards a twisting bridge
caught in the caress of
a mild earthquake

Medjool Dates

A narcissist
bending over
the holy waters
The pastor's assistant
her high cheekbones
still drop dead gorgeous at 65
placed the half wrapped
Styrofoam platter
on my desk

"Do you like dates?"

I peered over at the opened bundle
One third eaten
Medjool dates

The imagery started grinding
into my moment
These dry leathery dates
from some exotic
or temperate locale

quickly turned into crisp
cockroach carapaces

Each date tumbling
like the knobby fore knuckle of a dead man

So smooth and mulatto browned
Some whiff of mummification
riding the air above the dull fruit

The pastor's assistant picked out
and extended
one dry capsule
"I can't eat them all, you take these"

The dried-up quality
of her earnest offering
hung between us
as she
extended this fruit
from the blood red tips
of her flawless
manicured hand

She did not see me
watching her abstraction
Not once did she look at me

Accentuated by the grey-hued sky
picking up her reflection
in the window behind me
She could observe her features

These she watched closely
Carefully

Like a young woman
Tending another's baby

Hound

As I drive
toward my temporary situation
Past overly landscaped lawns
A powerful Alsatian
on the leash of a
nondescript man
lunges with intent
toward my vehicle

His wet fangs
appear artificially
whitened
These two have worked
together before

Each one
taking his turn
at the restraint

Grandfather and Rocko

Stood near the chain link fence
They glanced either down
or up
When deep thought
or cultural difference
held sway
They looked toward
the fig trees
Rocko had brought from Sicily
so many years back
Still covered in winter tarpaulin
and old tar buckets
two more old soldiers
making it through the winter

Grandfather
and Rocko
Would spit at each other
Bent Brooklyn words
Some Yiddish
Some Italian
Both speaking
and not speaking
Grandpa davening
Rocko spitting his words
and then spitting at the
fig trees
He was angry
as if the constant changes of time and care
and old rules dying out
and youth and fresh blood and new ideas
had done him in

I heard grandpa say
"But what'cha gonna do Rocko?"
What'cha gonna do?

And Rocko did it
He yanked the tarbuckets
from the fig trees
pulled their crooked arms
from their tarpaulin coats
He grabbed a firm limb
feeling along its course
for the life
and he said
"solo andare avanti fino
a quando non colpisce"

Just keep going…
Just keep going…
Until it hits.

From the Loneliness

In the early days
There were little lessons of kindness
or patience
Impossible to tell now
He slid the dry but still moving crab gently
off the pier
with the edge of his shoe
Silly black and whites were taken in the booth

I can see them now
Even though I gave him all the photo albums
All the photos
are eidetic and pounded into my stony memory

And there was adventure
Thousands of miles of it
But the drinking was hard
and he eyed the woman
And I drank alone next to him
sipping my loneliness thru the thin straw

Venice
The Caribbean
England
San Francisco
There were great distances to traverse
But he was a fast walker
and the bars always punctuated the sentences
that never existed between us

My way with words
The lariat of vernacular
I could rope and send to the skies
left him deaf and wide eyed
and the simple words
simply ignored

"I said I love you
Now go away"
Always punished
for getting too close

Patience became boredom
Boredom
Punctuated by crisis
Disasters, accidents
The mid-life bolt into
anything other than
growing together

And the nights after the babies were born
Were spent watching the black asphalt road
For his car

I cried from the loneliness
The tears turned into anger
You know the rest

Fool's Gold
Fourth of July

Sometimes we went to the chicken farm
Bottle rockets whizzing between the tires
of the black and white olds

Flatbush Avenue
Black and white cookies
and the sweaty line up for
the buses to the Riis Park beaches

Where I took off my top
And hoped for the best
A jug of alcohol
A Quaalude
Disco blasting
from every direction
Beach water
Cool as the hand
that never kept me

Dad loved the summer
The bite of a fresh
tomato held
hard in the fist

Halvah that nutty putty
Gritty in my teeth

And the hamburgers
grilled on the cement
on an electric barbecue
Awful

Yet significant
To the memories
Singing today

A mortal tsunami
will gather up its substance

And crash over me
one day

Until then
I am a potbellied old dream
Tearing herself away
from mediocrity
To look for fool's gold
on the roads to South Jersey

Endgame

Death comes on strong
Castrated and horned
Bellowing in some ear

And they sit up straight
and they say they cannot breathe
or catch it anymore

The drift, the sarcasm in the innuendo
The sacred shit we tell each other
before the mortal storm

Drugged or unconscious
No matter how you escape the sensations
of shutting down
Of leaving
the place of first birth

It will rise up in you
Shockingly so
You may be too tired
Too relaxed into it
to fully acknowledge
the wings fluttering at your eyelids
The lungs emptying, the purple feet

You will happen into this

You will

Happen

Into this

So why not empty into it

Let the soul cascade out
With a sparkle of awe
And a crash of expectation

Memorial Day

I know my limits
exceed the dreams I bear

The great graphics of
the American flag
The 5 radiating points
emanate invisibly from the celestial aspects

The Bars
Red and straight
White and horizontal
Match up and flutter
on those tiny tiny remnants
of the free life

I drag my dreams
across the cemetery soil
Past the granite markers
of those who have soldiered on

Everyone here has been
shot through by something
Lived through conflict and laughter

I reach the one I want

October 1, 2007

I did not expect
the wood paneling
the cleanliness
I thought the sad failings of the heart
should end abruptly
beneath bad lighting
amidst plasterboard
aluminum chairs and semi squalor
I did not expect the humanity

Gearing up this morning
The engine of my van faltered
and the uncertainty of the direction of the day
Like the chickadee at the courthouse granite pillar
began pecking at stone

Past the foggy cemeteries of
mini Mansions in development
Nestled low
where once, deer gathered

Past the dog on the leash
the taut leash

Past the radiology office
beckoning me to be free and clear

A red-faced man living it out
of his shopping cart
eyed my unsteadiness
"Jury duty" he said
"not really" said I
and then
he directed me

At the courthouse door

They took my pocket knife
Then I saw the others
And took my place on the bench

The bathroom
So clean
So unexpectedly inviting
in its sanitized way

And I looked in the mirror
The big judicial mirror
and it was only me there
I was whole, healthy
the same
breathing deeply

My lawyer
knows all the angles
knows the people, the rule
knows we are all the same
two becoming one
Friends becoming strangers
She talks of compassion
and the necessity of listening
I wish she was a god
teaching from the clouds the heavens
larger than life, thundering through
this place filled with endings

We sit here
all the voiceless circumstances
waiting for the moment to change
us for the better

The room fills up with sighs, and patience
good looking suits and spiked heels
It went quickly
efficiently, strong and clear
I put my palm on the black book of truths

Notes were taken
and the judge said good luck
No one sat at the other table
No one walked away but me

Slowly, lamely, I wandered back up the steep slope
of the parking lot ramp
I paused to look out over the concrete barrier
Out over traffic and the blue sky
Onto the unexpected poets house
Green shutters so much like my own

Those famous metaphors
Opening and shutting
against all known weather

I felt this way once before
Waiting for it to happen
in a veterinary hospital

With an old pet
Whose heart let me know
"It is time to move on"
Affection shared and claws bared
We could do it together
No longer

A woman looked at her
Waiting in her cage
"What a beautiful cat" she remarked

Afterwards
The sun was so very bright
And the day
Minus the content
Was so very beautiful

Amnesty

Strapped into
this hard beast of a seat
I enter the afternoons
delirium

With thoughts of hummingbirds pulsing
through sunlight energy

Isn't it enough
I gave myself on the rack to you
Victimized my soul
Buried by the paws of a scented dog
Denied and stuffed and denied
wide open possibilities
far from the cradle
the scrub brush and the hair brush?

There's no telling how far it will go
or where it will end up
It is endless and talking over
lines that have snapped
is impossible

Drenched in nature
my drug of choice
stars circle inside my head
drift down towards the pineal
sparking and releasing something
so full of hormones, molecules,
magic
and oblivion
possibility and prison

And the clock
Tick tocks

Marching music for the malady
of the grinding survival

Bad Breaks

She knew a lot
but she'd hardly learned anything
She specialized in nothing
but observed everything

Sometimes
Mechanical things broke
when she was around
Lightbulbs sparked and died

People came and went
Some moved on
Others flickered out
The ones still there
are waving back and forth

Waving at her
Tall grass
in dry soil

These are hard times
for the hearts

The Architect is Winking

I ran a mile today
Wounded bird
in a grey pastoral dawn
I showered
and went to work
Driving in
behind a white barn
I saw
a small wooden boat
haunches raised up on cinderblock

I saw this bobbing slowly
above the glimmer
of an ocean
beneath a bluebird's eggshell
colored sky
The delight and joy
of this pretty image
had me dancing
in the driver's seat

Earlier
on my way to the track
I asked for a sign
Maybe something coming in from the dead
Maybe a symbol
And the split second I finished asking
I saw it

Directed from a spray paint can
An orange day glow swash
Construction mark on the concrete

It gleamed up at me
Filled with an inner fire
It arched upwards

An arrow-like curve
and I felt I was being led
I lifted my eyes
and saw more
The pedestrian traffic image glowing white
on the crosswalk sign.

The white figure was walking
Walking

"Walk"
the architect said

So I did

Downsizing in Midlife

The young Puerto Rican contractor's assistant
asked me outright
"But what do you do for you"
and I couldn't think of any thing

He had taken his girlfriend to a Benihana
Where they sat ringside
to watch the knives flash
Onions roar up in sizzling flame
To catch the tasty morsels
on their tongues
as the Japanese chefs
tossed them at their patrons

I had been there and done that decades before
But I would not mention it
He showed me the video
of the restaurant experience on his cell phone

It wore all the bells and whistles
of an interesting night
Yet I was not stirred in the least

Am I too jaded
By years of high living
Exotic foods & travel
High and low beam art
and my daily dose of struggle

Am I depressed
and lingering

I didn't think so

"What do I do for me"

This

Flare

The bottom edges outwards
The linen curtains
flared out
Their ragged fingering edges
fluttering
A racy staccato arching
towards me

Waving in Pontifical blessing
"Learn the way" they say
"Learn how to achieve an uneasy
Peace already"

Endure

That tree
Bent horizontal
Split open
Nesting squirrels arch
against the fine lining
the inner fulcrum
of that drop dead
gorgeous dead hull

Endurance
will weed out the rest of us
When the heart attack comes
and it must
The tight fist
The broken shards
The clenched muscle
However it catches us
endurance will weed out the rest

It brings the lesson
When the chips are down
When the mask is off
Peace for the pain
Mirror to the narcissist
The shallow end is always reserved
for the fearfully shallow
Catch my drift?
That blank stare between the conscious
and the sleeping
The one who lunges forward
and the one who stayed the course

That tree
with its rhino horn
and bestial eye
Twice watches me pass

every day on my way
to such carefully paced
middle age aerobic reflections

Did I Give Up a Good Thing?

It doesn't feel like it
This yearning
for what we are supposed to fill ourselves
This hole we made

When we must close it
from within

I wonder about friendship
Difficult people appear
with the flaws we have lived with
over and over

Sometimes the smack of familiarity
resounds through another's mouth

People were sitting in my house
Small minded
Racist
Passive
Aggressive
and always having to win

I've lived in this hole
half my life

What do you do
What do you do

I don't want to win
Peace is always
a shut door away

People look at me
I look into people
Too much

Too often
Looking for the golden core

Finding empty children
Beating their chests
Mistaking this for a caress

Delaware Flood 2006

Now there is a Niagara
Barreling pressure
and foam
out of the mouth of a tremendous
thundering drain pipe
Widening
into the auburn mud
and whirling pools
of the famous Delaware

Gorged river
sounding of oceans
Heavy waves beating back
the mosaic-stone elbows
on this skimpy Titusville bridge

Extraordinary things are caught
against the steel cable underneath
ordinary things swirl by
I stand midway
between two histories
No one joins up
nor ventures out on foot
Just the rough vibration
of creeping motorists
moving on towards the safety
of the rest of their day

The air is ripe with
wet vegetation
a soccer ball heaves on by
a bobbing rotation
amidst the mahogany swells
It will be sometime
before the river and its banks
give in

Shove themselves away
after the hot sex of nature
and fold back in

In the meanwhile
park benches are in standing water
up to their planks
the barn and acre
half submerged
in the brown gold
will bear witness
to this moist and steamy event
producing jeremiahs
of dandelions next Spring

Now and then
the Delaware
has shuffled her decks
in this sienna manner
200 and 30 years ago
wide open like a woman
birthing for the 11th time

The British might have been
on the banks today
Raising a glass to the
hale and hearty
drum roll of
circumstance
and the wet pelt of fate

I feel the awareness
of the awareness of all of this
The literary dilemma
Everything rushing in at once
and the fear of the meaning evaporating
before it is written
The pearly rapids are everywhere

I leave the bridge and edge
downward to get closer

Where is everyone
Why is no one out to sea?
To feel?
The turbines of the Delaware
power up the natural history
of geography

On the river
ahead and behind
some things are broken on the outside
Some things
are broken
on the inside
I squeeze between the on ramp to the bridge
and a Patriots empty house
Below me
huge trees wallow out into the submerge

Fifty-pound bags
marked "balanced rations
Davis Feed Mills"
sandbag the pumpkin pine and hand forged doors
of this fieldstone house
Inside I can hear the remnants
of a woman praying
over other tragedies

There is no difference
between their prayers and ours
Only the quicksand shift
of time and circumstance
Sometimes on bended knee
Other times the knees
just buckle under

I love this house

here above the river
Permanence and good sense
High and dry on the hill
Anything rushing up this way
has been stopped in its tracks

Lower down
below the hill
Two-hundred-year-old trunks
kissed by the river tide
wear a smear of mud
stretching six feet
from root on up

And the islands
smack dead in
the walnut current
hold their own
one tree slowly waving
above the submerge

Planks drift quickly by
Bigger things
trawl the depths
their hidden selves
present as opacities on
calm surface waters

I move back and up
away from the new banks
slipping on the mud, the grass
and the wild wild ginger
The geese ahead of me
ruffle and flutter off
to feed near the house
in the shallow puddles

Ancient artillery are soaked
and the rush lights glimmer

River wood
River mud
It's all river now
across to the Jersey side
Deep and down there
A Titusville roofline
begins its 45-degree descent
into the moving murk
The house is full to the brim
It can hold no more

Many of us
choose to live on the edge
So ill defined
by the great levelers of all time
And it all keeps coming
above from New Hope
below to Trenton
All the little islands
awash with the sound
of one hand waving

We are still
Here
We still change the color of the landscape
We are broken beds being unmade
Waves and avalanches of current
shoot their arrows in the strength of this flood

New things hang from the boughs
of the biggest trees
still standing
Since all sorts of freedom
Set out across these waters

Cycling Past the Farm

The tire rims glisten
The rubber treads roll on
past oceans of sandy soil
currently awaiting a permanent wave
on out to the horizon

Behind the hollow barn
The pale blue motorboat
sits heavily on crumbling cinderblock

The eye of the mind
Readies it
Steadies it
to be set free
at the first sign of agriculture

The swarming of the vegetables
The waving in the sun

That boat will slip thru the reeds
like Moses
Crowned and anchored
by the moss
the weed
and all the accoutrements
of the growing season

Connect the Mortality

When I close my eyes to sleep
and just after I awaken
eyes not yet opened
I see it
The white dot
Hovering in the dark distance

The white dot has been there
for as long as I can remember
During periods of crisis and
canons of stress
it seems a tiny bit larger

But still small infinitesimal
On the distant horizon

The white dot
The reversal of period
The end of the metaphor

This morning I awoke
and after the exercise and the gearing up
as I washed out the rituals
I saw it

A red dot
Bright red
Blood in the chicken egg red
Left eye
Northwest of the pale green and gold pupil
I have admired for so long in the glass

Now the eye feels different
and I am testing my vision
Pulling the lid up
To see what will happen next

The red dot
scares me
The things I have learned
tell me it should not be
It is wrong
The things I have not learned
tell me it is ok

and that I am making good progress

Three days later
The red dot has been
reabsorbed and has
faded far away

The white dot
never leaves me
In the blackness surrounding it
white question marks whirl and swirl and
circle and funnel down through it
and out the other side
Speculation is endless

However
The dot emits nothing

But pure white light

Antiques

The value in any lesson
is where and how it cuts you

There is a wide plank pine door
When it swings open
with the rasp of ages

lindsey woolsey
and swigging ale
in the purple light of
poverty
are revealed

Hundreds and hundreds of days ago
of stockings and sour breath
The women are revealed
knowing nothing more
than nothing

And the kindly boot of man
H.M.S. Stalwart
rests under the bed

I want no part of this
the trappings
the rush lights
The dough scrapers and the
heavy hand
I turn away
I back out
The candles flare
into the pure light
of reasonable

20 Laurel

I hope the forces of irony
The gates clanging shut
The endurance for which I am not famous for
and all the rest of the green light virtues
will lift their grey wings
taking their heavy shelter somewhere else

My Dickinson yellow house
on the flat land that I will not go to see
for fear she will desert me
and fade into the dark matter
that holds all broken dreams

My golden house
With its small stand of bamboo
And a huge girthed ancient maple
waiting for me at the back edge of the garden
like a faceless man
A dark silhouette waiting for the introduction

This real estate deal
These lawyers, these realtors
These disclosures and negotiations
Solemn realities
reinforcing ourselves against
fraud and distrust
Insuring our rights our finances
and our agreements and our transfers
are in good repair and order

When all we really desire
is to share the passing
with good will
and exhausted by the wheeling and dealing
sit down to rest
in the new beginning

Talking

My heart
wants to forgive
as people
close off
and discard

I have one friend
She hears me
and quietly acknowledges
with a guttural sound

We let each other in
We argue with passion
Without anger
No one needs to win
This is new to me
I cherish this

Unexpectedly
an old friend called
The night I was laid off from the
work so seriously necessary
To keep the home
To keep my fragile sense of place

She sounds too calm
Laconic
Talks only of her work
She talks slowly
and placidly
only about herself

I wait to hear her say something of value
share some interest or empathy
I do not continue to ask her about herself

I know enough now to sense the self-absorption
The imbalance of interest

I know now how to end this kind of conversation
Graciously, thanking her for calling
She gets off the phone quickly
Did she sense the abruptness?
Did she scurry from rejection?
Who knows?

I am becoming proficient
in endings

I have become a success
in Silence
Appreciation
Tact and absurdity
And I proudly admit
That breaking me

Is quite the challenge

The Japanese Beetle

The Japanese beetle
Eats the green leaf
Turning it
into a tapestry
of brown lace

His gift
His talent
His nature
Is this

He knows just when to stop

Renfield

The time to give great voice is now
As people jump from windows
Through hoops
into caskets of alabaster
and bar codes

The time to march the unsaid
through the gutters
of the city
is here
in the palm of one hand touching another

A bastard's life is
as good as the rest

Two people
directly across the table
look into each other's eyes
Clarity is in there somewhere
Camera obscura the box
The damned box with all the labels and bells
Glass masks and the wicked dance
The images fuzzy or not at all

It's always the time to advance the cause
The reason is the size of knowledge
Knowledge is the size of ignorance and we all know
out of necessity

How ignorance massages the average intellect

Every tick tock of every second hand
messenger arranges the day
It's always sunrise and sunset
The hues hit the pineal
Fire in the works in the hold

In the belly
Every tick tock brings us closer to meaning
Or disparity

Put that renaissance halo on
And get to it

Nothing Here

Boys and girls are scared
to play outside
Because their brother was
killed right there for drugs or money
or nothing he got caught in the way
This is how it goes down
in most wars

Men with turbans
pump gas for the citizen
and the criminal

This ancient garb
has come to represent
Spirituality
and knocking terror
in the minds of those
waiting in the
automotive line-up

The beauty of money
comes only at the time it leaves you
In exchange by agreement or force
It has no morality
It is the way of ownership
of everyone and everything
that is bound and tied

Our dreams however
have no currency
Our dreams are just as out there
as the kid with the gun
or the guy with the golden goods
But because we reach out
of this known reality
to grasp them

and haven't mastered the art
We are stumbling over ourselves
Instead of regrouping
To try again

Our dreams
Our deepest desires
The sum of our
time here
is priceless
What we put here
moves forward into existence

We struggle to climb
the chain link fence
to escape the realities
we have created
Boogiemen are everywhere
In the back alleys, the gas stations
Stepping next to us
Doing double time

It is a true Halloween of the soul
out there
as boys do a jig
to keep one step ahead of the bullets
and the turbaned gas-pump jockeys
Praise Allah and count our damp
and wrinkled dollars
And everyone's leaders
raise the bar
on rhetoric and bad sense

Trade it all in
Hand it all back
Say I don't want this anymore
How
Do we give it all up?
Every single one of us

Must flash the consciousness of surrendering
to what is right
In our minds simultaneously
and wake up together

Will it happen?
Will it never happen?
Who's to say?
We have no wisdom
Nor sound judgement
No one has the belly for it anymore

Oh My Gawd

Some need to be broken by disease
The arrogant shining their predatory
searchlights
Loud and braying
into the depths of gentle souls

The sublimely entitled
Adrift on a current of
high expectation
These need constant pain
to brace themselves up against
Shoulder to the wall
of all for
Myself
Myself   Myself

Me Me Me all the god-damned time

Break the cowards
Those cowering bullies
Serve 'em up
Fill 'em with alcohol
curses and punches to the abdomen
Break 'em
The way *they* break 'em
Fast in and
Fast out
And then leave 'em

And break the gentle
The understanding and the compassionate
Break them on the white light
Tow them in
The wrecked and wretched barges
They tried so hard to understand it all
All the time

Sandbag those hulks

They break
All by themselves

Eye to Eye Over It

She makes faces when I tell her who I am
She gasps when I tell her what I did
She and her fiancée tell me how to eat
the delicious chicken
he has prepared
with his African spices.

"Eat it this way"
she insists
Placing the avocado slices
next to the chicken
in the sandwich.

I tell her I don't like avocado
even though I do
A childish stubbornness
is developing
That reeks of battles
with my mother.

"Eat it like this, you'll love it!"
She says again
When she was cutting it up
To save her the waste
I told her I did not like avocado
She cut up more and more of it
She told me I would love it.

When I ask pointed questions
She does not respond
When she tells me
Irish simpleton's jokes
I don't get them.

When we are together
The jagged edge of difference

shrieks up my ribcage
I need this friend
but cannot bear our friendship.

When she hands me the filthy dishrag
and looks me in the eye closely
gesturing towards the dishes
As if to say
"It's your turn, will you finish?"
I accept the challenge.

I tell her I am allergic to water
and I look her closely in the eye
The challenge is accepted
"Come now, and sit for some nice dessert"
"You'll love it!"

If I fall down
my steep sharp cellar stairs
Bruising myself on the
200-year-old stone walls
Breaking my head
on the concrete floor.

This willfulness will all be knocked
out of me.

And clean, and holy
I will smile with all
my facial muscles and shout "come in!"
When she rings the doorbell.

She Comes to Her Gelding

Muckers sucking Jersey clay
up to the calf line
The dishwater blonde
meets her man at the gate

His musculature is stunning
and spattered with mud
The cheeks and rump chipped away
Thoroughly assaulted
by an ongoing equine dispute
The conquest of territory and dominance
has held sway and had its way
nipping and tugging
at him
day after day

Domination and submission
stamp and snort
in this thin January summer
Statuesque field mates eye us
downwind
They eat us and know
we are nothing

We bring him to the barn
We are cooing and toning for him
in a strange way
His clip clopping and weighted gait
carries tremendous energy
But we still build his fences
He yanks his head up and down
over and over in my direction
The whites of his eye catch my own
He smells like carrot and celery
His thick lips tug at my sleeve

Women come here
to deal with
massive flesh and muscle
deep thick bone and weight
trying to get a handle on him

Fear and control
The lash and bridle
Tender restraints we apply
to insure submission

She works him weakly
on the lunge line
He is non-committal
easy in his way
he knows her inside and out
He is but a beautiful and weighty
beast at the end of his rope
he will apply himself
and end comfortably

She talks of the fear
that comes with age
and I hear the metaphor
for all the unknowns
that gallop thru our lives
she mounts him and begins

just a walk
then a trot

Nothing more
Anything less would be immobility
she knows this   so she keeps it going

The sun in January
is warm
The light is brittle and putty colored
I swing on the gate

And recall my little gone girl
Begging mommy for a horse
A massive strutting stallion
Something to begin with
My plastic pony trotted around my bedroom
My bicycle and saddle
Powerful between my childhood thighs
My hips and legs pumping
A racehorse's pistons
in full gallop on the Brooklyn
cement

We groom him together
I spray and detangle his clown red mane
work the clay off his cheeks and fetlocks
He raises his hindquarter
tilts his hoof
and places it on point
A small gesture of comfort
As I minister to him
I am content

My childhood dream of a Sunday
on the farm
Thoroughbred Mustang Palomino and Belgium Draft
Knicker and snort
Cobwebs and the
healthy stench
of manure and clay
all over me

When I leave here
I will not wash

Sending Out Vulnerability
Thank You for Protection

Holding onto
hard learned humility
Thank you for my consciousness
and progression

Feeling a strong integrity
Battling inner demons
Thank you for compassion from within

Allowing what comes around
to go
with the inner knowledge

and understanding that all psychic pain
is created from within

I bow my head
to your nature
Your silver tipped eagles
Your singing white birches
Your engaging silences
That speak louder than
the sounds of

Suffering
The cause of mutual damage

The sufferer
Who has purchased one ticket
and one ticket alone
shoves another
alongside themselves
Through the turnstile

Thinking they have gotten away

with something
However
They are only
on the other side
And will pass back through
Eventually and alone

The Dark Continent

In Africa
water is impure
and ebony skin
is marked
by the tracks
of mites
that have dug in
for the duration

My neighbor next door
is on her knees
vacuuming her lawn
one hyper-hand combs thru the grass
searching for errant debris

The other
obsessively clutches
the nozzle

The noise is deafening

God help me
I am not deaf

the suffering is everywhere

The Archetype

For Merlin

He was here
when we had no protection
The young boy put his arm around him
at night
Young boy
Big red cat

He was
not my choice
Chosen by one
Who could not commit to his care
or ours

Big red cat
He was our protector

At the open door
The window

His big silence
His indifference
His commitment to edging out the competition
at the food bowl

His flat out on his spine
beached whale splayed out resting position
So undignified for such a stolid unaffected beast

Yet on the rare occasion
We heard the growl rising up from the depths
to keep the strays at bay
To keep us inside
Together

He would not come when called
He did not like to be touched
The seven odd years before the shelter
seemed tinged with abuses
Neglect
The sins that petrify over time
had left their mark
But he became ours
and the bond was deep

In the end
he couldn't go without a little help

There was much talk
Many goodbyes
Nature sounds
and the loving protection
Of my young one and I
to carry him on his way

I am surprised at the depth of my grief
over this pet
This cat
This strong silent creature
whose vigil has ended

In our little world
Without our dreams and our furry friends

This hurts
Big time

Thank You House

This house
is about to release its hold on me
Its structure
and safety
Readying
for the new younger lives
Preparing as we say this
Happy am I to pass you on

My arms
that held babies
at night in these rooms
My arms that longed for what was always absent
In these rooms
are stronger now
Lifting the weight of material and change
has made them truly mine

This beautiful garden
Overgrown and heavy
needs new attention and care
My 250-year-old maple
beckons in the distance
My new friend
in my new space

I can't wait to leave
I don't want to leave
The tears come and go
The excitement grows

What will I make of my new home?
My new life
My latest and most present time
here on the surface of it all.

It is all here in my memory
This last settled morning's skies
are golden
Awash in revealing so little
and yet so much

The Tables Have Turned

The tables have turned on me
since the separation
Now I sit reception
and smile   smile   smile
I am in a holding pattern
of paychecks
Security cuffing my hands
behind my back
The calls peak at 2 p.m.
Fast voices push my responses
All manner of requests and issues
The building hums with importance
Everyone is on board

Today they are giving blood

The Romantic Outpost

The old woman
Alone on the road
No longer paved with beauty
and the mysterious promises

None are attracted
to her body any longer
Like a deflated balloon
It needs little
but a surface to lie upon

She is a romantic outpost
Wishing and sighing for
someone to know her
The way she knows herself
Yet knows this cultural myth
rarely occurs if at all

And if at all
The sacrifice
must be enormous and immortal

Her two miracles
Babies, toddlers, children, sons, men
Sleep on into the afternoon
She is full of illness
and full of cough and fatigue
Tottering back and forth
from one sleeping son to the other
Just to look

Amazed they are journeying with her
Upheld by their devotion
Crazy for their love

And finds it inexplicable

why they would be here
with her so weak and contagious
when they could be somewhere else
surrounded by youth, beauty, physical energies
and the mysterious promises

That all but broke her

ZAP

The urgency and direction
of spiritual lightning
in this dilemma
we call (whatever year it is)
is beating me over the head

It wants me to do something
Anything
Why it wants me I don't know
I didn't volunteer for anything
After all
I had just given up
Surrendered to the utter
pointlessness of practically
everything
except love and poetry

I'm muttering in my sleep
Mad angry surges of
exasperation
with the slow-moving currency of change
The uphill battle for a foothold
in any other direction at all
The news is no news
or bad news
The good news is
that we are still asleep

The sages of our time
are sleeping
Truth walks around the edges
of this room
Dark and silent as peace
Forefinger to the lip
Pensive
Serious

Oh so serious
Then the finger comes down
and we are picked

Most of us are picked off
But the ones who have to tell
the Truth
Sigh
And pick up their walking papers

On the Fringe

I am by all accounts
Living on the fringe
of my senior years

I have lived long enough
to have seen most of it

I swim in the senior community pool
with my dad
I ask him "can you still float on your back?"
He thinks I am asking him to teach
me how
and proceeds to instruct me
in the position and the way
I know enough
not to stop him

I only wanted to see him supine
eyes closed, lips flat lined
Floating away
in that last countenance of repose
So I could get a glimpse
of what is coming down
the road

Later on, with new found patience
I wait in my van
on the asphalt drive
at the insistence of my father

I cannot back out
until he has cleaned away
some bird droppings he had noticed
on the passenger side door
It seems very important to him
So very Ghandi

and I sit ashamed of my past behavior
in these sort of situations

As this is taking place
My mother
argues with him, a loud repetitious struggle
She has double thickness wipes in the kitchen
He found a single thickness roll in the garage
They pass in and out
of the kitchen doorway
He ends up confused
with her roll of paper towels in his hand
He heads towards the van again
The foot washing ceremony about to begin
on the passenger door side

Two dinosaurs
still battling for control
of the situation

Neither one
heeding to or acknowledging
the pointlessness of each other

This is the love
I grew up on

The cobra in the basket
Sometimes the lid is on
Sometimes the lid is off

You never knew when
the house was about to snap

The Eye of Osiris

This Linden tree
gracing the grounds
is full and bower heavy
Centuries of forest
and then placid oasis
have brought her to her knees
Egyptian endurance
through all that befalls us
in every aftermath
of time and weather

And early spring
attends to the inertia
at this institute for advanced study
Where quiet actions involving
rarified explorations
cross the slate paths
and linoleum hallways

The Linden bends
The sprouts from her grounded and rooted limbs
shoot up thick and full
and form trees of their own
tethered trees
mothered
wedded
enmeshed
you tell me

The inner journey
seems pure, and simple
on these monastic grounds
The complexities of scientific discovery

The right now of nature
Really says it all

From birth to grave
we move thru science and weather
I want to tell
how the boughs of this Linden
snake upwards in Medusa fashion
from the very base of her trunk

and the trunk
and the bellowing limbs
are each as thick as the other
and the solid limbs
branch out and far away

they lower
touch the soil
root and sprout
elephantine and serpentine
huge, huge branches

This Linden has never been pruned
or tormented by man or weather
Sitting adjacent to the battle field
where British and Colonists clashed and fell
centuries into it
This tree is magnificent
and now the leaves are coming

The inner eye may imagine
that somewhere
deep within her vital trunk
A lead bullet lies
A musket ball
Fired centuries ago

On the perimeter
of such an embedded thought
Little lives grow

The Appearance of Truth

The appearance of truth
bowled me over
Degrees of blades of grass
blowing timeless in the
authentic moments
The shimmers
The geysers
of enthusiasm
And ecstasy
edging in from the compass points
Unknowable
except when the soul is
ohhh so quiet

Entering into
the quiet room
Lined with moth's wings
and iridescence of spirit
so bright you can taste it
There is an exchange
of sensory experiences
on a mixed palette of
gifts and wishes

The room tastes like silver
The room feels like smiling

But then
that manly Quaker wind blows
friends are meeting and gliding by
sidling up to one another
and holding back
all the delicious and grateful
love and kindnesses
that could follow

They toss their hair
Brighten and edge forward
on a nervous harness
So earnest and edgy
with the song,
skip and dance

So I wonder
What to make
of the red balloon
of enlightenment

As it inflates
and deflates
The endlessly
magnificent
nothingness
waiting to take hold

We are well rounded out by
our experiences
If we will live to tell of them

The Softest Poem

The gentle queen size pleasures
Egyptian cotton skims a cheek
A pink feather falls on the lavender quilt
Taking its leisure and repose
next to the eye swiping ball of
sleeping fur and talented talon

I rest in my midlife tremors
Breathing the docile and epic sweetness
of my newness in my new spaces
My new faces and fragrant shimmers
wafting in from the history laden ancient yard

Sinking in sadness
had been the short boat
that kept me afloat
Until now
The rockets' red glare
and the angry past
Empty hulks with no storm to swirl
upwards and into

New furnishings
The new taste of water
from another reservoir and a new green glass to fill
So near and not so far
from the calm side of maturity

Episodes of melody and serenity
wash in through the windows
The honey tongue of loving it
with the life left for me
Drop by drop of savor and release
Minute by minute by minute

First Date

Where's the child?
I looked
Dinner was nice
First meeting
First glimpse

Where's the child?
I saw the glint in his eye
A moment
Like swimming alongside
a whale
A featureless wall
an emotionless eye
obscuring the depths
and we talked about mainframe computers

Where's the child?
I tried to see
during the concert
But could never catch it
His face
Older than mine
Broken harder by the same miseries
had fallen in upon itself
A collapsed star
Emitting little light
Deep folds of flesh
cast a veil over the window
that might have shown me
the true face of this soul

Craggy and pitted
Like the excavated side of a mountain

That face hardly smiled
It was a pleasant evening

When the Planks Were Laid Down

When the planks were laid down
and engaged to the process
with many square headed nails

They were aligned
and lined up alongside
and together
in a perfect manner
The effort and concentration
on making this
so admirable

In the beginning
The whirl of activity
The pressure of little lives
crossing over them
Had them creaking and
bending like the yellow willows
outside the bubbled windows

As time ate everything
They sang with a snap
Creaking thru winters compression
Softening and relaxing
as the spring came into orbit

These wide wooden planks
In this old house
Will
Given time
Decompose and fall thru

This is shaky ground
The floorboards are as good as our last honest step
before we fall thru
Science and religion want to know

about this
and edify us with the answers
And to what end it will all come to
after the wood is gone

Trenton

There was Yosemite
That grand arena
Redwoods and splendor
Everyone angling for the best
shot at it

No alarms went off
Small fires smoldered
around the begrudged gift
on the occasion of my 50th birthday

But those Redwoods at Muir
Led one to believe all was well
with the humidity and growth
along the restricted path

And the drinking
At last the drinking
between two old soldiers
almost friends
Near glances
darting off towards the
distraction of
geography and distance
Denial the sullen soup
the stale crust dips

And that last night
on the cusp of the Pacific
As I turned towards
the small possibility of intimacy
You were plain in your way
You wanted "one for the road"
and left the room
When you returned

the roadwork
was already underway

Back here in the County
Waiting for the other shoe to drop
When there was no other shoe
I stopped kicking myself
Came up for air

I break in Trenton these days
Far from the mist of Yosemite
Justice on my right
Poverty to the left
The Indian creek
flashing its silver minnows
I dip my shoe
where Washington's horses bent low
The healthy shimmer
cascades over my toe

The humidity amidst which
those redwoods thrive
Is up to its neck
in elements
minerals
Sulphur Dioxide
and the oooh and aahhh
of the innocents abroad

The leaves are gone
from our small stand
of wonder and puzzlement
The shallows in which their existence began
have overflowed into

My undeniable push
towards the unconditional

Perfume of the Injured

10 years angry
Never thought life's lessons would sink in
Just anger
That hard quartz
rutilated with hatred
and regret

Angry like a
Mistreated animal
And I was and am
My lions arm never raised to strike
So I lash out with the words
Spectacular words
They cannot understand

Ten years angry
Then he fell down the stairs
And I softened just a little
My great compassion for the injured
Rising up
The heady perfume of the love
for all damaged creatures

I heard of
the small deaths
Felt the pang when I saw the limp
and sorrow for the man who downed
the whole bottle on
the day of Thanks

He needed none of me
Made his joke
about his mismatched socks
Choked back a sob speaking
about his trip to Vietnam
And I still ached to know him

Still wished for it
whatever it was

My heart has unfurled
Into a difficult place
Now it is out of my hands
And I am not even waiting

People
are the people
who come to show us themselves
What we make of them
when love is lost

Is the love we lost

Pensive

This is not the work of
a mercurial artist
No swift linguistics here
Just a slow tongue
slapping the sides of the
jelly jar

Worms or eels
Squirming around
Sloshing the vowels

Understanding the
incomprehensible
is an easy day in the sun

Don't think too much
Unfurl the spirit antenna
Open the radar umbrella

Words can be
the string of pearls
worn to impress or gather in
the luminescent sensuality
of agreement or admiration

They can fill a singular locket
Then lock it away

They may just hang there
A pendant of thought
A vertical precipice of vernacular
waiting to fall from the lips

Like ice chips
or cherries
Either way
holds the communication

BIRTHDAY POEMS

54

Birthday poems always dance
in the sunlight
in the dark crevices
stumbling on weak ankles
over the dead
who turn like autumn leaves
into something wondrous

Pirouette over the selfish unloved
I danced around for centuries
until time and truth pried me loose
from the unhealthy moorings
I look back over the silver lacerations
of time and current

And kindly wave

The singular dance
and prance towards the grave
leads me away from logic
into the realm of the simple moment
This sad and wondrous expanse
of time and material
holds its hands out to me
and we caper off into the afterglow

Alone in the trembling dance
54 candles light the roadside
Graceful one moment
awkward lurch the next
Palm over each flame
as I dance by

My soul
presents herself
to each flair of warmth and color

Gratitude regret and expectation
whirl under the hooves
of white horses
with woman's buttocks

55

Still wet behind the ears
Wet noodle
Silly ska doodle
Awake in the wake
Smooth sailing ahead!

Will there be birthday noodles
or green nutrition?
A new major in my life
Padded and anchored
waiting to send me off?

My senior birthday
Hacking away at the marble façade
Michelangelo hunting for the gold inside
Let nothing and everything be discounted
Let nothing and everything be tasted
tested and discarded

Look at me
I said to 16 years old
Look at me and remember 55
Happy sad bold afraid
Changing my fashion, my ways
Stepping into the light linen
of mortality

56

I came into it
with forceps and the grip of white rubber
pressing down
Urgent without the word for anxiety
That would arrive much later
in an empty box
Wet and cold in the freezer of endurance
Warm up is what they meant
When they slapped me
Come on
Get with it
Dangling by the ankles
Pork on the hook
Next

Those were the days
when women knew it all
The shades were drawn and the bond
was nurtured without milk or honey
No peach fuzz sensuality of breast
The battle axe, the cloudy formulas
the boot and the leather strap
All that science and unconscious behavior could muster
Could hold up towards the light
in the test tube and the flask and exclaim
"It is good
It is what we all do"

And good it was
Adolescent colt
wearing the lily
the green carnation
the red rose of the soul

In the grip of the hallucinogens
spiraling thru the graveyard

The green wood
Learning a new profession
Donning the mask
The place and the procedures
Lowering the ceiling
Clamping the lid on tight

Not an ounce of authenticity was spilt
until the cement bond buckled under
the weight of
the lack of
and all the rest

The elephant backed away
saggy and tired
And I was left with new blood coursing
every which way

And every way is the right way
Every reality the right one
Wear it naked
If you try to fit into it
you will split at the seams
and cry
at inexplicable times
for no reason at all

57

I don't want to set the gravel
point the stones or mortar the damps
I am happy
in my ignorance
in my naïveté
and my dreams

The rabbits dance and twirl
in the back yard
Soon they will twirl for other dreamers

The trees I set
so lovingly in their beds
are healthy and their vibrancy
exuded fragrance
The whiskey breath of nature

The rooms become vacant and
whiter then the histories they held

The memories are moving
to a place inside me
They are stored in full color
Three dimensional
without sound and fury

My silent son on the phone
Happy Birthday shared
"I got nothing"
A generation apart
We try to span it
as best we can

The silences
Are where love is stored

58

Counting
Forsythia blooms
Acid yellow
Full volume

My voice is drying up
Drying out
My tongue
Dry leather
Flannel flapping in the wind

Potential seems unconscious
Oblivious to my pleas
Yet subtle changes
seem to please me

Me
so small
so hidden
So tall
So well formed

I dance with aging graces
Embrace and embellish
Twirling into my colors
Grey hair and green eyes

I never wanted so much, so much
Life was all I could ever, could ever
Beautiful momentary life
The harmonics of sundown shadows
and gentle warm breezes

I am surrounded by
broken and damaged vehicles
I cannot fix them, it hurts me to try

They punish me for trying

One eye
Looking at me
with spiritual love
could help heal the gash
in my heart

That eye
offended
has been plucked out

Acid yellow forsythias
Edvard Munch- black and white scream
hiding in there

The seat of my soul is on fire
Consumption sets in
Phoenix arise

59

Springtime
and forceps
brought me in

The breath
once so shallow
alternates between
deep credence in all that is

And shallow holdings
based on lack of self-assuredness
mistakes, forgetfulness
And the extreme fear of what others
may or may not be able to see

My routines
are solitary
The solitary poet
building an arc of word
some wisdom
such fear
all based on the dire outcome

I am too naïve
too alone
too hopeful
too trusting

Afraid my stupidity
will land me in a mental hospital
My job my livelihood
feel like my last chance
to sustain an empty reality
based on apprehensions

Where do we go?

for the unconditional love
lost to us early on?

Do we ever stop yearning for it?
I cannot tell
No one talks to me
I talk out loud to myself
I talk to the tree
the wind and the water
I spread my yearnings
and my aloneness over the elements
like butter on bread
licking any wound that presents

I feel the need to
surpass my failures
to implement success
where inadequacy holds sway

I pat my shoulder, caress my cheek
I correct my posture
I would give it all up
for the honest hug of loyalty

Typos abound
I correct those too
and move forward
Always…

into the backwardness of
an oblivion that is neither here
nor there

A thought just occurred
maybe I can correct the problem
if I think it through
Clearly

Clearly…

61

The thick smattering of happiness I had
frescoed on to my persona held fast
and made a happy birthday

The vibes like radar emanated all over
The glint of the mercury waves and the tinkle of the
ice cubes in the current of tomato justice and vodka
wrapped themselves around my giddy naiveté
that for so long has been my anchor to God
Or whatever started up this game of chance

It's great here
I can dig my toes into the granular sand
The indecision of choice
massages my heels as we walk towards stale memories
It's really glorious
The book of life is open I can rip those early chapters out
and toss them onto the endless embers of heartbreak and loss
I can lift the earth and pour all the oceans onto that fire
and still it smolders
and smirks at my constant attempts to get past
what in profound essence is really
just my life

Oscar Wilde
had it the worst way
Nothing could touch his abandonment
But he had wit and style
And when it all left him
with an earache and a French death
his last words still sparkle
in the deathbed writhing

"I cannot stand this wallpaper…one of us will have to go."

I have come to this sandy spot
nothing to toss in

Decorate no one as per chapter 2
Rearrange no furniture
as I was instructed in chapter 6

Now the broken book is light
And the chapters are candles
by the side of the sea

62

The particular pleasures of older age
have opened my synapses
and brought me to the knees of some great oak
with seven trunks
and a safe house with seven histories
Tucked into its walls, timeline and company
and in part to all those to whom reparations are
due, from a humbled me...

A humbled me shambles on...
Still full of the strengths of life
and conviction
Still full and shot through with it all
The music
The wisdom
and the disciplines needed
to speak to all the above

Yet,
They are a long time
and a hard road
Baring down and paring
away all the illusions
Some need to be kept close
If stripped away
may lead to such a raw reality
that death draws near
and dying is such a raw reality

the hard breathing
the rattle of the last exhalation

Like athletes bursting through the finish line ribbon
The reality, the relief and exhaustion
at having made the run

64

I've been hob knobbing with obscurity
Dancing in her circles
Sipping in
and not posting anything

Barely able to conceal my disdain
for the multitudes of success
sucking the media teat

The people
are proving themselves
My obscurity is proof
of my own dark success
and now I am here

I face my demons silently
I delve into the mysteries
with my eyes closed
My head bowed

The feeble constructs of personality
fall away
All the new age quotes, slogans,
mantras and visualizations
Pale

My dead father
peers wistfully my way
in his folding chair
by the door

All I want is the time and space
that is left
to sit in the folding chair
I have opened
Perch up and forward

into the sun and the light
Shifting into low gear
and horizon bound

The Last Poems for My Father

Transition

Overlooking the beautiful hospital landscape
My aged Alzheimer Father
pinches and gestures in his twilight dementia

His aim is true
Yet he has to sidestep the purple and blue hallucinations
and the litter from the heart attack that caught him unaware
that second day in the hospital

He is angry and hardly lucid
Fiercely babbling his expressions full of incoherency
Small bursts of the hardest absolutes, pellets of bewilderment
Trying to make sure and hateful at the impossibility

I come around by 5
It is my 59th birthday
And I would so like to hear his voice
See his smile, and be warmed by his acknowledgement
But he never wakens
I hold his hands and brush his forehead
Put a tender palm upon his chest
and feel once again so young

Remembering the same vignette
that took place at the sofa where he rested
on Saturdays in 1963
I once was the child fixing his pillow
Waiting for his affection

The love from 54 years ago fills me today
As the scene replays in my head
A sphere of memory that can rise to the surface
whenever I wish it

I go to the large hall window to cry
brush back my tears and look out again on all that springtime beauty

This natural and grief laden transition fills me once more
Keeps me positive and in the moment
Things may improve
The end will certainly come

These things I know
and breathe in like fire
My nostrils are red
My eyes inflamed
The hills of Princeton roar with color
My aged Father sleeps the deep profound sleep
of entering into some small healing
the all points compass of white light
either one or both

We all become spheres of memory
for others to hold up to the white light
This sphere, this planet of time and past
is filled with dark continents
light rivers of bonding and intimacy
Weathered moments
and this…

It's as simple
as that

At Dad's Grave on Father's Day

In 4th grade
I brought him handkerchiefs

Monogrammed in red
He smiled
even though I never saw them again

Through the years
There were ties
and gloves
Pistachio nuts
So very many pistachio nuts

The sound of them cracking open
between his teeth
A half century old transmission
coming through
by virtue of a
musical synapse

Radios
Black handballs
Spalding pink balls
Tennis balls
Ping pong balls

We ran
We caught
them flying by

He hoped for athletes
But he got us instead

Fatherhood begins in hope
And winds up in love
With sons

And daughters

Whose sweetest gift was
to wish to be in his presence
on Father's Day.

Upwind

The horses knew
I was afraid
The address was true
but the location
a breeder's farm for racehorses

I was looking for mulch
To keep new life
from growing up out of the topsoil

I was afraid
I thought of my newly dead Father's hand
reaching up out of his topsoil
My grasping it
and pulling him back through

Out and upright
The only way I knew him

I talked to two of the
racehorses
Sleek, huge
with mullet manes
and no flies
Well-tended from hoof to muzzle

I said to them
I said "Now I am afraid
I am afraid of everything
I am even afraid of you"
My childhood dreams
My favorite creatures

I could not read them well
Lost to the few
who truly loved me

I could not read them
and I told them this

One by one the small herd came over
Heads bowed, hindquarters working
They stood near me
Ears forward
Breathing it all in
Nipping each other on the neck
The ear
Swinging low to gnaw blue fescue
or a solitary flowering field onion
The small bud of life's beauty
at the end of the stalk

I told them about my sadness
and then, feeling emptied
slowly walked my sixty years of this
back towards the car
Parallel and somber
along the wooden rails
they walked with me
Keeping my pace
Their heads dipping and divining
Holding my silence

I wondered where their ancestors were
Where all ancestors are
and was calmed and set alright in
some small way
by their attention
and their finite consciousness
A flashlight, a moment,
so timeless and apparent
On and off
And then it was gone

We held each other's attention
Is that not what it is all about?

E.R.Beirne shares many of the themes other poets have explored. Nature, death, the journey of the self, victimization, musings on the body and the love between mother and child. Born in Brooklyn N.Y. her life has been filled with the intertwining's of Art, Music and Literature.

Through her years as a Manhattan based Art Director and Graphic Artist/Book Designer/Illustrator for the Publishing Industry and the Brooklyn Museum of Art, as well as managing her own design studio – Blue Heron Graphics, E.R. Beirne has enjoyed a lifelong romance with the Arts. Singing and playing guitar in NYC and New Jersey has allowed her to participate in another passion, Music. She has been a Poetry Editor/Book Designer for The East River Review and has written poetry and short stories since the age of 6. This is her first endeavor into publishing her own work.

"It is poetry, and all expressive writing, that speaks for the soul, both individual and universal, expressing the inner voice developed over a lifetime of self-talk and profound contemplation."

E.R.Beirne